QUICK, SMART GRAMMAR
ADVERB

Developed by

Neeti Kaushik
Post Graduate (Education)
(Active in the field of education
for the past 14 years)

Anamika Dutta
Post Graduate (English Literature)

Neeti and Anamika are involved in developing creative and interactive reading material for children. They have also authored books on Environment, Life Skills and Preschool Concepts.

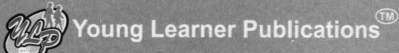
Young Learner Publications™

Contents

GRAMMAR SCRAPBOOK:

Punch and tag a few sheets of art paper into a booklet. Use old greeting cards to make the cover.

RESOURCES:

Use pictures from old books, magazines, newspapers, posters and greeting cards. Check out some smart ideas given in the book!

Printed at: Deewan Offset, Delhi
© Young Learner Publications

Adverbs and Their Types

What is an adverb?

An adverb is a word that modifies:

- a verb
- an adjective
- another adverb

Examples

The nightingale sang sweetly.
         ↓   ↓
       verb adverb

The soldier marched smartly.
         ↓   ↓
       verb   adverb

He owns a very expensive car.
       ↓   ↓
     adverb adjective

The traffic moved quite slowly down the road.
         ↓   ↓
     adverb adverb

Kinds of Adverbs

There are seven main kinds of adverbs.

- Adverbs of Degree
- Adverbs of Time
- Adverbs of Frequency
- Adverbs of Place
- Interrogative Adverbs
- Adverbs of Manner
- Relative Adverbs

Use of Adverbs

Adverbs make sentences more informative. They are used:

- To say how:
  The dog barked <u>loudly</u>.

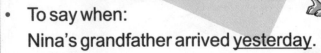

- To say when:
  Nina's grandfather arrived <u>yesterday</u>.

- To say where:
  The children are playing <u>outside</u>.

- To say how often:
  Rahim attends school <u>regularly</u>.

- To make the meaning of an adjective, an adverb or a verb stronger or weaker:
  The day was <u>extremely</u> cold.
  Her mother scolded her <u>mildly</u>.

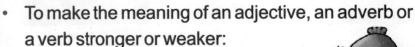

Adverbs which modify verbs

Many adverbs end with the suffix -ly. Most of these are created by adding -ly at the end of an adjective, like this:

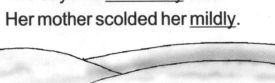

ADJECTIVE	ADVERB
Slow	Slowly
Beautiful	Beautifully
Careless	Carelessly

However, this is NOT a reliable way to find out whether a word is an adverb or not, for two reasons: Many adverbs do NOT end in -ly (some are the same as their adjective forms), and many words which are NOT adverbs DO end in -ly (such as kindly, friendly, elderly and lonely, which are adjectives).

Here are some examples of adverbs which are the same as adjectives:

ADJECTIVE	ADVERB
fast	fast
late	late
early	early

Understanding

The best way to tell if a word is an adverb is to try framing a question, for which the answer is the word. If the question uses how, where or when, then the word is probably an adverb.

Examples

Word in context	Question	Adverb or not
Sania plays tennis **swiftly**.	How does Sania play tennis?	Yes, uses HOW.
They have a **small** car.	What kind of car do they have?	No, uses WHAT KIND OF, so this is an adjective.
The manager called the police **immediately**.	When did the manager call the police?	Yes, uses WHEN.

The most frequently used adverbs are too, so, really and very. In fact, these words are often overworked. To make your speaking and writing more interesting, replace these general adverbs with more specific ones, such as completely, especially and quite.

PRACTICE

A. Given below is a list of adverbs. Put each adverb under the correct heading.

> today, tomorrow, kindly, upstairs, neatly, there, outside, inside, later, sweetly, quickly, angrily, never, early, downstairs

How	When	Where
....	....	....
....	....	....
....	....	....
....	....	....
....	....	....

B. Use adverbs to answer the following questions.

1. When are you going to your grandparents' house?

   _____

2. When will you do your homework?

   _____

3. Where are the keys?

   _____

4. How do you clean your teeth?

   _____

5. Where are your books?

   _____

6. How did your neighbour talk to you?

   _____

Understanding

An adverb of time tells us the time when an action took place. To identify it we can ask a question starting with "when".

Examples

Eat your lunch now.
("now" - Adverb of time)

I have never worked before.
("never" - Adverb of time)

I will go to the library tomorrow.
("tomorrow" - Adverb of time)

Word List

late, just, next, soon, now, still, later, today, nights, tonight, finally, mornings, evenings, already, recently, tomorrow, afternoons, currently, yesterday, eventually, afterwards

PRACTICE

A. Rearrange the words to make sentences and underline the adverbs of time.

1. haven't/recently/seen/I/Sara

   _____

2. I/you/will/talk/later/to

   _____

3. soon/go/will/to/we/Malaysia

   _____

4. Noddy/already/I/met/have

   _____

5. has/letter/finally/the/reached

   _____

B. Underline the adverbs of time.

1. She came yesterday.
2. He is planning to visit us tomorrow.
3. She will be playing the match today.
4. Afterwards he was sorry for what he had done.
5. Rosy represented her team then.
6. The cargo finally arrived.
7. Peter eventually learnt to solve the sums.
8. I will be going to the mountains soon.
9. Steve has already been to the circus.
10. Doctor Maria is still in the operation theatre.

Adverbs of Place

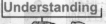

An adverb of place tells us where the action was carried out. To identify it we can ask a question starting with "where".

Examples

There was snow everywhere. ⟶ "everywhere" - Adverb of place

Shiny did not want to go there. ⟶ "there" - Adverb of place

Word List

here, there, home, abroad, outside, nowhere, anywhere, aside, elsewhere, upstairs, somewhere, underground, northwards, westwards, eastwards, southwards, upwards

Many **adverbs of place** also function as **prepositions**:

up, by, off, in, next, over, besides, across, under, behind, around

GRAB A GRAMMAR FACT

Adverbs of place are usually placed after the main verb or after the object:

Examples

after the main verb:
- The cat looked away/up/down/around.
- I'm going home/out/back.

after the object:
- They built a hut nearby.
- He took the child outside.

PRACTICE

A. Fill in the blanks with suitable adverbs of place.

1. The kitchen is _____.

2. We have been looking for you _____.

3. There is a bucket lying _____.

4. We could not find our puppy _____.

5. The boys were studying _____.

B. Underline the adverbs of place.

1. Noddy stayed here for a week.

2. We could not find John anywhere.

3. Miss James has just gone out.

4. The painter painted the picture there.

5. We are going abroad next month.

6. Mary stays upstairs.

C. Use the adverbs you underlined above to make sentences of your own.

1. _____

2. _____

3. _____

4. _____

5. _____

6. _____

Understanding

Most adverbs of manner are closely related to the corresponding adjectives. Although some words can be used as either adjectives or adverbs, in most cases, adverbs of manner are formed by adding 'ly' to the corresponding adjectives. To identify them we can ask a question starting with "how" or "in what manner".

Spelling rules for adding 'ly'

In most cases, 'ly' is simply added to the positive form of the adjective.

Examples

ADJECTIVE	ADVERB OF MANNER
bad	badly
complete	completely
normal	normally
surprising	surprisingly

Adjectives ending in 'ic'

When the adjective ends in 'ic', the syllable 'al' is usually added before the 'ly' ending.

Examples

ADJECTIVE	ADVERB OF MANNER
dramatic	dramatically
scientific	scientifically
specific	specifically

Adjectives ending in 'le'

When the adjective ends in 'le' preceded by a consonant, the final 'e' is usually changed to 'y', to form the 'ly' ending.

Examples

ADJECTIVE	ADVERB OF MANNER
favorable	favorably
humble	humbly
simple	simply

When the adjective ends in 'le' preceded by a vowel, in most cases, 'ly' is simply added to the positive form of the adjective.

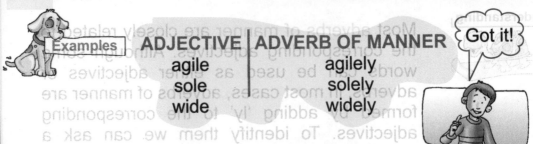

Examples	ADJECTIVE	ADVERB OF MANNER
	agile	agilely
	sole	solely
	wide	widely

Got it!

EXCEPTION! In the case of the adjective whole, the final 'e' is removed before the suffix 'ly' is added.

ADJECTIVE	ADVERB OF MANNER
whole	wholly

Adjectives ending in 'll'

When the adjective ends in 'll', only 'y' is added.

Examples	ADJECTIVE	ADVERB OF MANNER
	dull	dully
	full	fully
	shrill	shrilly

Adjectives ending in 'ue'

When the adjective ends in 'ue', the final 'e' is usually omitted before the suffix 'ly' is added.

Examples	ADJECTIVE	ADVERB OF MANNER
	due	duly
	true	truly

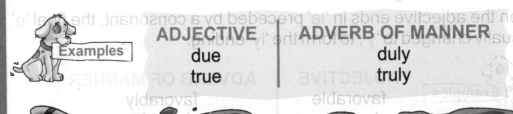

Adjectives ending in 'y'

When the adjective ends in 'y' preceded by a consonant, the 'y' is usually changed to 'i' before the suffix 'ly' is added.

Examples

ADJECTIVE	ADVERB OF MANNER
busy	busily
easy	easily
happy	happily

EXCEPTION! In the case of the adjectives shy and sly, the suffix 'ly' is simply added to the positive form of the adjective.

ADJECTIVE	ADVERB OF MANNER
shy	shyly
sly	slyly

When the adjective ends in 'y' preceded by a vowel, in most cases, the suffix 'ly' is simply added to the positive form of the adjective.

Examples

ADJECTIVE	ADVERB OF MANNER
coy	coyly
grey	greyly

Rare
Rarely

Usual
Usually

Lucky
Luckily

PRACTICE

A. For each of the following sentences, fill in the blank with the adverb that corresponds to the adjective given in brackets and rewrite the sentence.

> **HINT**
>
> | Adjective | Adverb |
> |-----------|----------|
> | calm | calmly |
> | strong | strongly |

1. Mandy sings _____ .(sweet)

   _____

2. The little boy behaved _____ . (naughty)

   _____

3. Mr John can _____ (quick)
   solve crossword puzzles.

   _____

4. The black horse ran _____ . (swift)

   _____

5. Jack got hurt_____ . (bad)

   _____

6. Hannah dances _____ . (graceful)

   _____

7. Dalton speaks _____ . (confident)

   _____

8. The water flowed _____ . (rapid)

   _____

9. The boy played the guitar _____ . (loud)

   _____

10. The thieves whispered _____ . (soft)

    _____

B. Replace the underlined words with adverbs of manner and rewrite the sentences.

1. The doctor dealt with the emergency <u>with calmness</u>.

   _____

2. Iqbal dribbled the ball <u>with skill</u>.

   _____

3. Nancy answered the questions <u>with honesty</u>.

   _____

4. He shut the door <u>with anger</u>.

   _____

5. He was colouring the picture <u>with neatness</u>.

   _____

C. Put the following adverbs of manner in sentences of your own.

clearly, gladly, sharply, properly, loudly

1. _____
2. _____
3. _____
4. _____
5. _____

I am writing the sentences in my Grammar Scrapbook and drawing some cute pictures too!

Adverbs of Degree

The doctor dead with the emergency with calmness.

Understanding

An adverb of degree tells us to what degree, extent or intensity something happens. To identify it we can ask a question starting with "how much".

Examples

The poor man was **terribly** hungry.

"terribly" - Adverb of degree

A cheetah runs **extremely** fast.

"extremely" - Adverb of degree

Word List

too, very, so, quite, almost, really, greatly, highly, totally, hugely, enough, extremely, perfectly, gratefully, partially, immensely, adequately

Balanced perfectly!

PRACTICE

A. **Fill in the blanks with suitable adverbs of degree.**

1. The students were _____ confident.
2. We enjoyed our holiday _____.
3. This professor is _____ respected.
4. They are _____ prepared to meet the challenge.
5. The hill was _____ steep and difficult to climb.

B. **Underline the adverbs of degree in the following sentences.**

1. The lamp was too hot to touch.
2. Mary knows me quite well.
3. The dinner was absolutely delicious.
4. She hardly works.
5. Dorothy is a highly skilled operator.

C. **Tick (✓) the correct options and complete the sentences.**

1. The garden is _____ beautiful.
   a) immensely ☐
   b) almost ☐
   c) enough ☐

2. I am just _____ exhausted to work any more.
   a) too ☐
   b) very ☐
   c) enough ☐

3. Is this suitcase light _____ for you to carry?
   a) too ☐
   b) very ☐
   c) enough ☐

4. Thank you _____ much for your kind help.
   a) too ☐
   b) very ☐
   c) enough ☐

5. Do you have _____ ration for emergencies?
   a) too ☐
   b) very ☐
   c) enough ☐

6. We should eat a _____ balanced diet.
   a) perfectly ☐
   b) really ☐
   c) too ☐

7. Don't worry about your father; he'll be home _____ soon.
   a) too ☐
   b) very ☐
   c) enough ☐

8. This is an _____ complicated issue.
   a) so ☐
   b) too ☐
   c) extremely ☐

9. We don't get enough time to play because we have _____ much homework to do.
   a) too ☐
   b) very ☐
   c) enough ☐

10. This television set is _____ expensive.
    a) adequately ☐
    b) highly ☐
    c) gratefully ☐

Adverbs of Frequency

Understanding

An adverb of frequency tells us how often an action is carried out. To identify it we can ask a question starting with "how often".

REMEMBER

These adverbs are usually placed after or before the simple tenses.

Examples

He is **always** present.

"always" - Adverb of frequency

We **sometimes** meet them.

"sometimes" - Adverb of frequency

I am **generally** at home in the mornings.

"generally" - Adverb of frequency

They should **often** visit them.

"often" - Adverb of frequency

I exercise **regularly**.

"regularly" - Adverb of frequency

Word List

daily, often, rarely, weekly, monthly, annually, always, seldom, normally, regularly, generally, frequently, sometimes, occasionally, periodically, hardly, ever, almost, never

PRACTICE

A. Rewrite the sentences placing the adverbs of frequency in the correct place.

1. He is late for work. (usually)

   _____

2. Teak is used to make furniture. (sometimes)

   _____

3. I have been to Paris. (never)

   _____

4. The fees must be paid. (quarterly)

   _____

5. She visits her grandparents. (often)

   _____

B. Underline the adverbs of frequency in the given sentences.

1. The flight is seldom late.
2. Peter could never win a prize.
3. I play tennis occasionally.
4. The train is normally on time.
5. James is never angry.
6. Pedro is often ill in winter.
7. I hardly ever travel abroad.
8. I usually like to have porridge for breakfast.
9. I often go to the cinema with my friends.
10. Cyrus appears on the channel frequently.

Relative Adverbs

Understanding

A **relative adverb** modifies a noun or a whole sentence. "When", "where", "why" and "how" are relative adverbs.

Examples

I remember the day **when** we first met.

"when" - Relative adverb

Tell me **why** you are looking so scared.

"why" - Relative adverb

The street **where** I live is congested.

"where" - Relative adverb

I don't know **how** they arrived.

"how" - Relative adverb

Relative Adverb	Meaning	Use	Example
When	in/on which	refers to time	The day when she met her.
Where	in/at which	refers to a place	The place where she met her.
Why	for which	refers to a reason	The reason why she met her.
How	in what way	refers to a manner	The manner how she met her.

PRACTICE

A. **Fill in the blanks with suitable relative adverbs.**

Hard work brings success.

1. This is the place _____ I was born.
2. I do not know _____ they left so early.
3. That is the reason _____ he is so successful.
4. _____ the prisoner escaped has always been a mystery.
5. There was a time _____ there was hardly any traffic on this road.
6. This is the station _____ Clara met Sam.
7. July and August are the months _____ most people go on holiday.
8. Do you know the reason _____ so many people in the world learn English?

LEARN ENGLISH

9. This is the church _____ my parents got married.

10. Edinburgh is the town _____ Alexander Graham Bell was born.

11. 25th December is the day _____ children get their Christmas presents.

12. Famine was the reason _____ so many villagers emigrated to the neighbouring land.

13. A greengrocer's is a shop _____ you can buy vegetables.

14. It is this time of the year_____ we hold a family reunion.

15. A horror film was the reason _____ I couldn't sleep last night.

B. Underline the relative adverbs in the following sentences.

1. I know the date when my great grandfather was born!

2. This is the time when you should start studying.

3. That is the ground where the cricket match is going to be held.

4. The reason why he left the school is not known.

5. I shall tell you about the shop where you will find a lot of books.

Interrogative Adverbs

Understanding

An interrogative adverb is used to ask questions.

Examples

When is the school reopening?
"When"-Interrogative adverb

Why don't we go for a walk?
"Why"-Interrogative adverb

Where have you been?
"Where" -Interrogative adverb

How can I help you?
"How"-Interrogative adverb

PRACTICE

A. Underline the interrogative adverb in each sentence.

1. How much does the bag weigh?
2. Why did you choose not to go?
3. When do you want to come over?
4. Where have all the birds flown?
5. How many pencils do you have?

B. **Fill in the blanks with appropriate interrogative adverbs.**

1. _____ did you disobey your teacher?

2. _____ many storybooks have you read?

3. _____ don't they dig the soil?

4. _____ have you kept the car keys?

5. _____ high is the prison wall?

6. _____ don't they ever finish their work on time?

7. _____ old is your younger brother?

8. _____ have you kept your bag?

C. **Paying attention to the correct word order, rewrite the indirect questions as direct questions.**

For example:

I wonder how often it rains here.

How often does it rain here?

1. I want to know how much money you collected for the charity.

   _____

2. I wonder where they were.

   _____

3. Tell me why I should attend the wedding.

   _____

4. I would like to know when he finds time for his family.

   _____

5. I wonder why she left the theatre.

_____

6. I am curious to know how many times you have seen this play.

_____

7. I want to know when you completed the project.

_____

8. I want to know how long it will take.

_____

9. Tell me where Andrew is.

_____

10. I wonder why the shopkeeper did not reply.

_____

11. Find out when the bakery opens.

_____

12. I wonder where Mr Federer is staying.

_____

FOR YOUR GRAMMAR SCRAPBOOK

Jot down the recipe of your favourite dish. Encircle the adverbs and name them. Your mother would love to help you out with this!

26

Adverbs which modify adjectives or other adverbs usually come just before the words they modify.

Examples

The tower is <u>extremely</u> <u>tall</u>.

extremely : Adverb
tall : Adjective

The Robinsons' had a <u>badly damaged</u> house after the storm.

badly : Adverb
damaged : Adjective

Chelsa proudly displayed her <u>carefully</u> <u>embroidered</u> sheet.

carefully : Adverb
embroidered : Adjective

The furniture that they sell is <u>fairly</u> <u>sturdy</u>.

fairly : Adverb
sturdy : Adjective

Some adverbs of manner, place, time and frequency have the same forms as the corresponding adjectives.

Examples

Adjectives	Adverbs of Manner
Fast	Fast
Hard	Hard
Little	Little
Loud	Loud or Loudly
Much	Much
Straight	Straight

Adjectives	Adverbs of Place
Far	Far
High	High
Low	Low
Near	Near

Adjectives	Adverbs of Time
Early	Early
First	First
Late	Late
Long	Long

Adjectives	Adverbs of Frequency
Daily	Daily
Monthly	Monthly
Weekly	Weekly
Yearly	Yearly

PRACTICE

Insert the adverbs correctly and rewrite the sentences.

1. Smith was in China. (recently)

   _____

2. He visits the church. (rarely)

   _____

3. The old man waited. (patiently)

   _____

4. My mother does the cooking. (always)

   _____

5. There are four bedrooms. (upstairs)

   _____

6. He goes to the gymnasium. (regularly)

   _____

7. Bats can hear. (well)

   _____

8. I have heard this music. (before)

   _____

9. Arif spoke on the topic. (eloquently)

   _____

10. Charles is prepared for the competition. (fully)

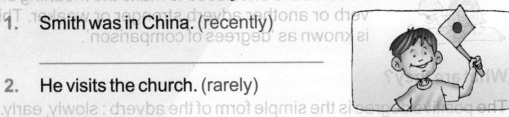

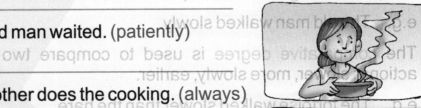

Understanding

Adverbs are often used to make the meaning of a verb or another adverb stronger or weaker. This is known as 'degrees of comparison'.

What are they?

The positive degree is the simple form of the adverb : slowly, early.

e.g.   The old man walked slowly.

The comparative degree is used to compare two actions : slower, more slowly, earlier.

e.g.   The tortoise walked slower than the hare.

The superlative degree is used to compare three or more actions: slowest, earliest.

e.g.   They all take their time, but Robert works the slowest of all.

In general, comparative and superlative forms of adverbs are the same as for adjectives:

add -er or -est to adverbs:

ADVERB	COMPARATIVE	SUPERLATIVE
hard	harder	the hardest
cheap	cheaper	the cheapest
fast	faster	the fastest

Examples

- Simi works harder than her brother.
- Everyone in the race ran fast, but Catherine ran the fastest of all.

For adverbs ending in -ly, we use more for the comparative and most for the superlative degree:

ADVERB	COMPARATIVE	SUPERLATIVE
quietly	more quietly	most quietly
carefully	more carefully	most carefully
seriously	more seriously	most seriously

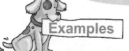

The guide spoke more clearly to help us understand.

Could you sit more quietly please?

Some adverbs have irregular comparative forms:

ADVERB	COMPARATIVE	SUPERLATIVE
badly	worse	worst
far	farther/further	farthest/furthest
little	less	least
well/good	better	best

- The naughty sheep ran further than its flock.
- Today you are reciting worse than last week!

EXCEPTIONS! Sometimes 'most' can mean 'very':

- We were most grateful for your help.
- I am most impressed with this application.

Adverbs may function as intensifiers, conveying a greater or lesser emphasis to something. Intensifiers have three different functions: They can emphasize, amplify or tone down.

Examples

- I really don't believe you.
- He literally wasted his father's money.
- She simply hates non vegetarian food.
- They're surely going to be on time.
- He spoke quite firmly to him.
- They almost forgot about the function.
- The judge completely rejected her appeal.
- I absolutely refuse to attend any more late night parties.
- They heartily endorsed the new line of clothes.
- I somewhat like this idea.
- The ship was literally ruined by the storm.

WORKSHEETS

A. We can completely change the meaning of a sentence by changing the adverb. Here is an example:

The kids were dressed neatly.

The kids were dressed untidily.

Change the meaning of these sentences by replacing the adverbs.

1. The man spoke rudely to the children.

_____

2. Granny walked slowly through the orchard.

_____

3. She always kept her belongings carefully.

_____

4. Roger talked confidently in the class.

_____

5. The car moved rapidly on the highway.

_____

B. Find the adjective in the first sentence and fill the gap with the adverb.

1. Jessica is happy. She smiles ....
2. The man is loud. He shouts ....
3. Edburg's English is fluent. He speaks English
   ....
4. Our teacher was angry. She spoke to us
   ....
5. My uncle is a careless driver. He drives
   ....
6. Tim is a wonderful guitar player. He plays the guitar
   ....

7. This girl is very quiet. She keeps on working ....

8. She is a graceful dancer. She dances quite ....

C. **Read the sentences carefully and tick (✓) the correct options.**

1. What is an adverb?

   a) An adverb gives more information about the noun.

   b) An adverb gives more information about the preposition.

   c) An adverb gives more information about the verb.

   d) An adverb gives more information about the sentence.

2. Which adverb would you use to complete the following sentence?

   The tightrope walker walked _____ on the rope.

   a) awkwardly

   b) carefully

   c) skilfully

   d) heavily

3. Which of these sentences does not contain an adverb?

   a) The dog ran happily towards his master.

   b) Simon walked to the bank.

   c) The babysitter gently picked up the sleeping baby.

   d) She met her cousins yesterday.

4. Which of these words in the following sentence is an adverb?

   Snow White looked longingly at the gate, waiting for the friendly dwarfs to be back.

   a) looked

   b) longingly

   c) friendly

   d) dwarfs

5. Which of these statements about adverbs is incorrect?

a) We use an adverb in place of an article.

b) We use an adverb to say how often something happens.

c) We use an adverb to say when or where something happens.

d) We use an adverb to say how something happens.

6. Which of these adverbs tells you how something happens?

a) early

b) carefully

c) inside

d) later

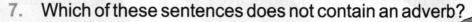

7. Which of these sentences does not contain an adverb?

a) We are leaving tomorrow.

b) We walked swiftly.

c) I bought a pair of boots.

d) She dressed smartly for the interview.

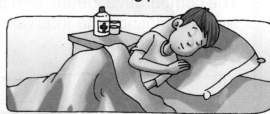

8. Which sentence has the adverb in the wrong place?

a) Suddenly he felt sick.

b) He suddenly felt sick.

c) He felt suddenly sick.

d) He felt sick suddenly.

FOR YOUR GRAMMAR SCRAPBOOK

Collect cut-outs of adverbs for each letter of the English alphabet from old newspapers. Paste them in your grammar scrapbook.

ABROAD   BEHIND

Adverbs and Adjectives

Adverbs and adjectives have some common characteristics. However, an important difference between the two is that adverbs do not modify nouns.

ADJECTIVE (✓)	ADVERB (x)
Maggie is a *happy* child. (✓)	Maggie is a *happily* child. (x)
Maggie is *happy*. (✓)	Maggie is *happily*. (x)

The following words (with their comparative and superlative forms) can be both adverbs and adjectives: early, far, fast, hard, late.

Let us use 'early' both as an adjective and adverb:

ADJECTIVE	ADVERB
I'll catch the early bus.	I woke up early this morning to catch the bus.

The comparative 'better' and the superlative 'best', as well as some words denoting time intervals (daily, weekly, monthly), can also be adverbs or adjectives.

Understanding

Adjectives that do not change form (or add -ly) to become adverbs are called flat adverbs.

Examples

early, late, hard, fast, long, high, low, deep, near

To decide whether these words are functioning as adjectives or adverbs, we must find out :

1) What the word is describing (noun or verb).
2) What question the word is answering.

Examples

'Early' as an adjective:

Hercule Potter caught an early train to his hometown.

'Early' describes the noun 'train' and answers the question "which?"

'Early' as an adverb:

Sam arrived early the next day.

'Early' describes the verb 'arrived' and answers the question "when?"

'Hard' as an adjective:

He is a very hard taskmaster.

'Hard' describes the noun 'taskmaster' and answers the question "what kind?"

'Hard' as an adverb:

The master made the slave work hard.

'Hard' describes the verb 'work' and answers the question "how?"

PRACTICE

In each of the following sentences, indicate whether the highlighted word is an adverb or an adjective:

1. My school bus arrived LATE, as usual.
   Adverb ☐   Adjective ☐

2. I will be studying till LATE night.
   Adverb ☐   Adjective ☐

3. My elder brother loves FAST cars.
   Adverb ☐   Adjective ☐

4. She talks too FAST.
   Adverb ☐   Adjective ☐

5. This sum is HARDER than I thought.
   Adverb ☐   Adjective ☐

6. I feel it will rain HARDER today.
   Adverb ☐   Adjective ☐

FOR YOUR GRAMMAR SCRAPBOOK

Find eight adverbs each for: eating, walking, laughing and writing. You may follow the format given below.

ANSWERS

PAGE 6

A. HOW: kindly, neatly, sweetly, quickly, angrily.
WHEN: today, tomorrow, later, never, early.
WHERE: upstairs, there, outside, inside, downstairs.

❖ **Suggested Answers :**

B. 1. I will be going to my grandparents' house tomorrow.
2. I will do my homework later.
3. The keys are inside the drawer.
4. I clean my teeth properly.
5. My books are lying upstairs.
6. My neighbour talked rudely to me.

PAGE 8

A. 1. I haven't seen Sara <u>recently</u>.
2. I will talk to you <u>later</u>.
3. We will <u>soon</u> go to Malaysia.
4. I have <u>already</u> met Noddy.
5. The letter has <u>finally</u> reached.

B. 1. yesterday   2. tomorrow
3. today   4. Afterwards
5. then   6. finally
7. eventually   8. soon
9. already   10. still

PAGE 10

❖ **Suggested Answers :**

A. 1. downstairs   2. everywhere
3. outside   4. anywhere
5. upstairs

B. 1. here   2. anywhere
3. out   4. there
5. abroad   6. upstairs

PAGES 14-15

A. 1. Mandy sings sweetly.
2. The little boy behaved naughtily.
3. Mr John can quickly solve crossword puzzles.
4. The black horse ran swiftly.
5. Jack got hurt badly.
6. Hannah dances gracefully.
7. Dalton speaks confidently.
8. The water flowed rapidly.
9. The boy played the guitar loudly.
10. The thieves whispered softly.

B. 1. The doctor dealt with the emergency calmly.
2. Iqbal dribbled the ball skilfully.
3. Nancy answered the questions honestly.
4. He shut the door angrily.
5. He was colouring the picture neatly.

PAGES 17-18

❖ **Suggested Answers :**

A. 1. very   2. immensely
3. quite   4. fully
5. extremely

B. 1. too   2. quite
3. absolutely   4. hardly
5. highly

C. 1. immensely   2. too
3. enough   4. very
5. enough   6. perfectly
7. very   8. extremely
9. too   10. highly

PAGE 20

A. 1. He is usually late for work.
2. Sometimes teak is used to make furniture.
3. I have never been to Paris.
4. The fees must be paid quarterly.
5. She often visits her grandparents.

B. 1. seldom   2. never
3. occasionally   4. normally
5. never   6. often
7. hardly ever   8. usually
9. often   10. frequently

PAGES 22-23

A. 1. where 2. why
 3. why 4. How
 5. when 6. where
 7. when 8. why
 9. where 10. where
 11. when 12. why
 13. where 14. when
 15. why

B. 1. I know the date <u>when</u> my great grandfather was born!
 2. This is the time <u>when</u> you should start studying.
 3. That is the ground <u>where</u> the cricket match is going to be held.
 4. The reason <u>why</u> he left the school is not known.
 5. I shall tell you about the shop <u>where</u> you will find a lot of books.

PAGES 24-26

A. 1. How 2. Why
 3. When 4. Where
 5. How

B. 1. Why 2. How
 3. Why 4. Where
 5. How 6. Why
 7. How 8. Where

C. 1. How much money have you collected for the charity?
 2. Where were they?
 3. Why should I attend the wedding?
 4. When does he find time for his family?
 5. Why did she leave the theatre?
 6. How many times have you seen this play?
 7. When did you complete the project?
 8. How long will it take?
 9. Where is Andrew?
 10. Why didn't the shopkeeper reply?
 11. When does the bakery open?

 12. Where is Mr Federer staying?

PAGE 29

 1. Smith was in China recently.
 2. He rarely visits the church.
 3. The old man waited patiently.
 4. My mother always does the cooking.
 5. There are four bedrooms upstairs.
 6. He regularly goes to the gymnasium.
 7. Bats can hear well.
 8. I have heard this music before.
 9. Arif eloquently spoke on the topic.
 10. Charles is fully prepared for the competition.

PAGES 33-35

❖ **Suggested Answers :**

A. 1. The man spoke kindly to the children.
 2. Granny walked swiftly through the orchard.
 3. She always kept her belongings carelessly.
 4. Roger talked nervously in the class.
 5. The car moved slowly on the highway.

B. 1. happily 2. loudly
 3. fluently 4. angrily
 5. carelessly 6. wonderfully
 7. quietly 8. gracefully

C. 1. c 2. c
 3. b 4. b
 5. a 6. b
 7. c 8. c

PAGE 38

 1. Adverb 2. Adjective
 3. Adjective 4. Adverb
 5. Adjective 6. Adverb